Original title:
Beneath the Brambles

Copyright © 2025 Creative Arts Management OÜ
All rights reserved.

Author: Riley Hawthorne
ISBN HARDBACK: 978-1-80567-255-5
ISBN PAPERBACK: 978-1-80567-554-9

Veiled in Vines

Tangled up like a lost sock,
I tripped over a vine and knocked the clock.
Giggling flowers peeked out to stare,
They whispered secrets with wild flair.

A hedgehog rolled by, wearing a hat,
Mumbling about things that aren't where they sat.
With every step, I danced with glee,
In this wild waltz of greenery free.

Echoes of Entangled Roots

Roots do a jig, 'neath the old oak tree,
They laugh and they groan, what a sight to see!
With squiggly rhymes and a tap-tap sound,
They outdance the squirrels all around.

A rabbit with flair hops by with pride,
Claiming he's the best, no secrets to hide.
But tangled he gets—oh, that silly hare!
Guess the roots thought it'd be fun to share!

Cursed Corners of the Grove

In a corner where the wild things mix,
A chicken found plans to do some tricks.
With feathers all ruffled, it took a stance,
Declaring it's time for a forest dance!

A llama rolled in, wearing shades of green,
Said, "What a mess! This place is unclean!"
The trees shook their leaves in fitful laughter,
As creatures gathered, running faster after.

Hidden Paths through the Green

Where paths twist and turn, a giggle takes flight,
Banana peels lie waiting for night.
A gopher in glasses adjusts with a grin,
Saying, "Watch out folks, slip and spin!"

A snail named Sally, with a crown so bold,
Claims she's the queen of all things uncontrolled.
In this tangled web, we laugh and cheer,
For the hidden paths bring us all so near!

Echoes from the Underbrush

A squirrel sneezed, the leaves did shake,
A rabbit jumped, a funny quake.
The hedgehog giggled, rolled in glee,
A party held beneath the tree.

The fox wore shoes, the owl wore hats,
They danced with glee, like silly brats.
The snails brought snacks, a feast so bright,
While crickets played tunes deep in the night.

The raccoons clapped, their paws did cheer,
While butterflies swirled, with laughs to hear.
A lizard juggled, oh what a sight,
As fireflies danced in the fading light.

But with dawn's arrival, laughter ceased,
The critters scattered, their fun released.
Yet echoes linger in the mist,
Of underbrush joys we can't resist.

The Veil of Leaves

In leafy cloaks, the critters creep,
They sneak and peek, not making a peep.
A bear in disguise, a hat too big,
Stumbles and tumbles, oh what a gig!

The rabbits scheme, they plot and plan,
To trick the owl, oh what a fan!
A wig of twigs, a tail of reeds,
They giggle and laugh as humor leads.

The moles hold court, in shadows they sit,
Cracking old jokes, thinking they're it.
A chorus of chuckles, a raucous cheer,
As shadows dance, and laughter's clear.

But hidden beneath their playful prank,
A wise old turtle, with clever flank,
Plays tricks of his own, a merry fling,
While the forest chuckles, let joy take wing.

Enigma of the Twisted Vines

Twisted vines form a puzzling sight,
Like twisting tongues in the soft twilight.
A chameleon sings, "What's up with that?"
While squirrels think they've found a hat.

Beneath the tangle, a bumblebee,
Wears a crown made of leaves, like royalty.
The ants parade, they march with flair,
In search of crumbs, they trample where?

The owls hoot riddles, in night's dim glow,
"Why did the leaf fly?" Oh, just for show!
A riddle wrapped in a viney twist,
As fireflies flash, they truly exist.

Each turn conceals a giggling sprite,
Who tickles the toes of the unwary night.
A laughter echoed beneath the leaves,
Where mischief plays, and joy believes.

Frosted Petals in the Understory

Amidst the frost, the petals gleam,
Like candy jewels, a sweetened dream.
The hedgehog swirls, a ballroom king,
In winter's dance, with a happy fling.

A mouse in mittens, with tiny feet,
Leads a waltz, oh so discreet.
The robins chirp in silly tune,
While snowflakes giggle, a soft cartoon.

A snowman pranced, with carrot nose,
A jolly fellow, who often goes.
He slips and slides, "Oh, what a mess!"
But laughter rings, and he feels blessed.

As sunlight warms the frosty ground,
Each creature gathers, joy all around.
With petals bright, the day takes flight,
In a world of fun, where all is light.

In the Grit of the Undergrowth

In the thicket, critters play,
A raccoon steals the picnic tray.
Squirrels giggle, hiding nuts,
While worms discuss their muddy ruts.

A hedgehog dons a tiny hat,
Plans a party with a chat.
The flowers dance, their petals twirl,
As beetles waltz, their shells all swirl.

The Murmur of the Obscured

Amidst the leaves, a secret's told,
A snail once dreamt of striking gold.
The spiders weave with wily grace,
While ants hold court, a bustling place.

The shadows chuckle, misty and sly,
As butterflies flit by to say hi.
The wise old owl, with glasses perched,
Reads the gossip that's long been searched.

Whispers of the Shaded Realm

In shadows deep, the shadows prance,
The mushrooms sway as if in a dance.
A caterpillar cracks a joke,
While tree frogs croak and play tote-a-roke.

With every rustle, secrets bloom,
The bushes giggle, clearing the gloom.
A gopher thinks he's quite the star,
But trips on roots, oh, how bizarre!

Of Roots and Tresses

The grass sings low, a verdant tune,
While daisies gossip under the moon.
A chipmunk juggles acorns with flair,
Squeaking laughter fills the air.

A squirrel in shades shares wild tales,
Of nutty quests and windy gales.
The moss, all soft, begins to snore,
While crickets crack up, longing for more.

Rustling Tides of the Wilderness

In the woods where critters cheer,
Squirrels scatter, drawing near.
They plot and scheme, a busy crew,
While trying to outwit the shoe.

A raccoon dances on a stump,
With feet that make the forest thump.
He doesn't know, but we all see,
He's got a knack for tasty brie.

The owls hoot with a wise old tone,
While foxes sneak with a cautious groan.
An acorn drops, and all freeze fast,
Nature's chaos – unsurpassed!

The sun dips low, the shadows stretch,
A turtle's slow, but never wretched.
With laughter echoing through the trees,
The forest plays its jovial tease.

The Lure of Unseen Corners

In corners green, where mischief brews,
Tiny fairies don their shoes.
They giggle as they toss a leaf,
Creating chaos, sparking grief.

A snail, in style, moves oh so slow,
He's in no rush, just watching go.
While beetles race, they trip and fall,
And blame the wind for the great sprawl.

Hiding rocks engage in chat,
Singing songs of an old hat.
The shadows twist, the mushrooms laugh,
In corners where the unseen craft.

So come and play in nature's game,
Where nothing's quite the same, the same!
With jests and jives from dusk till dawn,
Adventure calls—let's carry on!

A Symphony of Twists and Turns

The path ahead winds round and 'round,
Where playful mischief may abound.
A hedgehog wears a crown of weeds,
While plotting all his regal deeds.

With every curve, a joke is flung,
A chipmunk serenades, forever young.
While crickets chirp in rhythmic glee,
And dance along in jubilee.

Each tumbleweed rolls with flair and twist,
Making sure that none are missed.
The leaves applaud, the branches sway,
Encouraging the frolic play.

So join the tune, let laughter soar,
In nature's hug, there's always more.
With a wink and a nod, we spin and twirl,
In this wild world, merrily whirl!

Nature's Enigmatic Embrace

Underneath the twisted vines,
A wise old frog, observing signs.
He croaks a riddle, full of cheer,
As fireflies dance without a fear.

The branches creak a rusty song,
Encouraging the critters strong.
With every twist, there's room for play,
Secrets lurk in blossoms' sway.

A mischievous breeze plays chase and run,
As rabbits hop, having their fun.
The trees gossip with a rustling sound,
While flowers giggle at what's found.

In nature's grasp, we laugh and jest,
Every day brings a quirky quest.
With laughter echoing through the space,
Life blooms bright in this warm embrace.

Where Thorns Meet Love

In the garden of care, there's a prickly delight,
Where roses and laughter are never polite.
With giggles and pokes from each thorny embrace,
We tango with shrubs in a wild, quirky race.

With humor we navigate this bushy domain,
Sharing secrets with daisies, avoiding the pain.
Who knew love could bloom in such tangled up places,
A dance with the thorns leaves us smiling with graces.

The Hushed Harmony of the Shrubs

In the bushes, the whispers of farce fill the air,
As squirrels plot antics that vanish with flair.
The bushes shake gently, each chuckle, a tease,
While flowers conspire with a giggle and sneeze.

Amidst leafy dilemmas, the critters unite,
In a comedic ballet beneath shadows of light.
Nature's own sitcom plays out with great flair,
As we laugh at the chaos and join in, if we dare.

The Timelessness of Tangled Trails

Through pathways entwined, where the wild blossoms bloom,
We tumble and stumble, but never feel gloom.
With vines wrapped around us, we dance without care,
A forest of giggles, we breathe in the rare.

With each twist and turn, there's a chuckle and cheer,
Nature's own circus where all of us hear.
The trail may be tangled, but joy sees us through,
In these quirky adventures, there's always a new.

Choreography of Leaf and Light

In the flicker of sunlight on leaves, we find glee,
With shadows that twist, like a lively jubilee.
The branches perform in a whimsical sway,
As laughter erupts in this leafy ballet.

Each rustle and ruffle is a step in our play,
With critters as dancers, they join in the fray.
In a world full of whimsy and quirky delight,
We dance through the sunlight, a soft comic sight.

The Secret Language of Foliage

Whispers in the leaves, they say,
Telling tales of yesterday.
Squirrels gossip, trees confide,
In this green world, we can't hide.

Rabbits chuckle at the jest,
Their twitching noses, oh so blessed.
While owls roll their wise old eyes,
At jokes only the wind supplies.

Mushrooms dance with glee on roots,
In their finest leafy suits.
Ants march on, a tired crew,
Wishing for a break or two.

Caterpillars plotting schemes,
In the thick of leafy dreams.
Nature's humor, loud and clear,
Bringing laughter year to year.

Within the Forest's Embrace

In the woods where shadows play,
Trees have secrets of their way.
Bunny ears perk up with cheer,
As chipmunks crack a joke or sneer.

Sunlight tickles through the leaves,
A comedic dance that never leaves.
The fern's a comedian, quite spry,
Making mosses laugh as they sigh.

Branches stretch to touch the sky,
While vines hang low, oh my, oh my!
They twist and wind, like laughter's spout,
In a nature show we can't live without.

Underneath a canopy bright,
Fungi giggle in the light.
With a chuckle and a tease,
Forest friendship brings such ease.

The Painters of Green and Gold

Brushes dance in a mossy glade,
As sunbeams paint a cheerful shade.
Golden leaves, like laughter, fall,
Creating art, a joyful sprawl.

Frogs provide the croaky song,
As they leap back and forth along.
A canvas stretched with nature's hand,
Colorful antics, oh so grand.

Breezes giggle through the pines,
While dandelions dance in lines.
Together in this vibrant jam,
Life is silly as a clam.

With each stroke, we paint our days,
In greens and golds, in quirky ways.
Nature's jesters, bold and bright,
Laughing with hues of pure delight.

Beneath Canopies of Untamed Beauty

Underneath the leafy shade,
Nature crafts a funny parade.
Branches wave with playful grace,
While breezes blow and tickle face.

In the underbrush, chaos reigns,
As raccoons play their silly games.
Twisting roots like jester's bows,
In laughter's realm, joy freely flows.

Critters greet the morning light,
With antics that spark sheer delight.
Hiding behind thickets, they stare,
With mischief twinkling in the air.

Among the vines and wild surprise,
Silly bats flutter like wise guys.
In this wild world of whimsy grand,
Every creature lends a hand.

Soliloquy of the Hedgerow

In the quiet nook where critters scheme,
A hedgehog whispers to a dreaming stream.
"Oh, to be a bird and fly so high!
Instead, I stick to this patchy pie!"

The rabbits laugh and dance with glee,
While chatting squirrels sip their tea.
"What a life, beneath the leaves,
Finding nuts and dodging thieves!"

A wise old tortoise takes a seat,
As ants march by in perfect beat.
"You silly beasts, just wait and see,
I'll win this race quite leisurely!"

And so they muse, a merry band,
In a world that's wild and quite unplanned.
With every chuckle, every jest,
The hedgerow thrives, it feels quite blessed.

Secrets of the Sturdy Stems

Oh, the stems that twist with playful pride,
Each leafy secret they surely hide.
The flowers gossip in colors bright,
As bees buzz by with pure delight.

"Did you hear the tale of the lazy vine?
Climbs so slowly, thinks it's divine!"
Giggling daisies wiggle with cheer,
While thistles mock with pointy sneers.

Frogs croak jokes from the murky muck,
"Why don't trees ever give a duck?"
As laughter ripples through the air,
A band of blooms breaks out in flair.

Secrets shared among the green,
Life's absurd, but what a scene!
A world so silly, we can't complain,
Where joy blooms wild, like sweet champagne.

The Heart of the Untamed Thicket

In the tangled mess of vines and grass,
A critter fumbles while trying to pass.
"Watch your step!" calls a teasing hare,
"You'll land in trouble—or in the air!"

The brambles chuckle, embracing the fun,
As shadows dance in the afternoon sun.
"Who needs a path when you can roam,
And bump your head on a leafy dome?"

A parade of insects strut their stuff,
With tiny hats and a dance that's tough.
"Step to the left and twirl around,
In our wild thicket, laughter is found!"

So they frolic, tangled yet free,
In a world where every moment's a spree.
With giggles and jests as the day slips away,
The heart of the wild invites here to stay.

Veiled in Verdant Shadows

Amidst the ferns in shades of green,
A grumpy gnome is seldom seen.
"Why must the sun interrupt my nap?
These flowers giggle, they deserve a slap!"

But roses sway and begin to tease,
"Join our dance, you'll surely please!"
With stubborn frown and a wobbly jig,
He stomps about, then starts to dig.

The mischievous snails begin to race,
While pollen floats, it's a chaotic place.
"Oh no!" he cries, as friends draw near,
"This verdant veil hides way too much cheer!"

In shadows deep, where laughter swells,
He learns that life's best at giggles and yells.
So here he stays, lost in his plight,
Veiled by laughter, in the fading light.

A Labyrinth of Leafy Whispers

In the garden where squirrels play,
Leaves whisper secrets in a funny way.
A snail races past, what a curious sight,
While the flowers giggle with pure delight.

A hedgehog dons a tiny bright hat,
While a bird tries to chat with a fat little cat.
The bees take selfies, indulging the ruse,
As petals play poker with nothing to lose.

The Elysium of the Thicket

In the thicket where shadows play cheeky games,
A rabbit wears glasses and calls out names.
A fox in a tutu dances quite bold,
While the trees clap their hands, never growing old.

The toads hold a concert under the moon,
With croaking applause, they're quite the tune.
Fireflies jive in a mischievous way,
Leaving trails of giggles at the end of the day.

Embracing the Natural Twine

Twisting pathways where jesters abound,
A raccoon recites vows to the ground.
The vines reach out like fingers of fun,
As ladybugs giggle, embracing the sun.

A caterpillar's dream of becoming a king,
While grasshoppers chant, ironically sing.
A lizard with swagger claims all he can,
While the flowers roll eyes, such a humorous plan.

The Poetry of Petals and Prowls

In the soft light where colors collide,
Petals write verses with nature's pride.
A mouse dressed as Shakespeare takes a bow,
While daffodils smirk, "What's happening now?"

A bear in pajamas wakes with a snore,
As shadows conspire to play, dance, and roar.
The breeze brings laughter, a joke in its trail,
In this wild kingdom where whimsy prevails.

The Whisper of Thorns

In a garden where the thorns like to play,
They tickle my ankles and make me sway.
The roses gossip, the daisies delight,
As I tiptoe through laughter under moonlight.

The squirrels in suits hold a crazy convention,
Debating if nuts are the ultimate invention.
The prickly plans hatch amidst leafy cheer,
I can't help but chuckle at all I hear.

The thistles wear crowns made of rust and jive,
As they dance with the weeds, feeling quite alive.
With snickers and giggles from petals so bright,
This thorny party is quite a sight!

So next time you wander in gardens of glee,
Watch out for the prickers, they'll sneak up on thee.
For while flowers may bloom, and petals may flirt,
Watch where you step or you'll end up with dirt!

Hidden in the Greenery

In the bushes where the mischief unfolds,
A hedgehog in glasses reads scandalous scrolls.
The ferns wave their arms like they're smitten with style,
While snails debate fashion in a slow, silly dial.

The daisies have secrets they giggle to share,
While the grasshoppers host a snack time affair.
With crumbs of sweet cookies and juice from a pear,
Who knew nature's children could party with flair?

The bumblebees sing in a chorus so loud,
As they joke about plants and how they've been plowed.
With each pitter-patter of gentle spring rain,
The laughter of critters can't be contained!

So venture in softly, with mischief in mind,
For nature's a joke that's hilariously blind.
In bushes and brambles, wild stories ignite,
With confessions from creatures beneath starlit night.

Secrets of the Enchanted Grove

In the grove where the magic plays peekaboo,
A mischievous sprite stole my shoe, it's true!
The old oak chuckles, its branches swing low,
As I chase after laughter in twinkling glow.

The mushrooms whisper of stories untold,
Of pixies and fairies, both crafty and bold.
I spot a fox rolling in leaves like a pro,
With a toad as his partner, they steal the show.

The flowers wear glasses and gossip away,
While the wind shares a tale of a clumsy jay.
With giggles and twirls, the fireflies play,
Dim lights in a theater, come join the ballet!

In this grove where the secrets of nature reside,
Laughter and fun are the things we abide.
So come dance with the shadows and sing with the beams,

For the grove is alive, bursting forth with dreams!

Tangle of Nature's Embrace

In the tangle where vines weave a silly snare,
I stumble and trip, my shoes in despair.
The vines giggle softly, they love a good fall,
As I tussle with thickets that seem to stand tall.

The critters convene for their daily parade,
While chattering trees poke fun, unafraid.
With acorns for hats and twigs for a tie,
They march in a line, oh my, oh my!

A butterfly flutters, a jester so bright,
Tickling the petals, a whimsical sight.
And over the hill, I hear wild rabbits cheer,
Wagering on who'll win—last hop, my dear!

So if you should stumble in nature's tight grip,
Just laugh with the leaves, take a comedic trip.
For amidst all the tangles, so wild and absurd,
The giggles of green life are the best kind of word!

Thickets of Forgotten Dreams

In a thicket where dreams seem to hide,
A squirrel named Ned took a wild ride.
He danced with a bee, oh what a sight,
While the thorns laughed and tickled with delight.

The bushes whispered secrets, silly and bold,
As berries juggled thoughts of stories untold.
Ned twirled in circles, a daring young chap,
Till a thorn snagged his tail, oh, what a mishap!

With a chuckle and grin, he untangled his pride,
While the bramblefolk cheered, "Come join in," they cried.
In the thicket of folly, with laughter so pure,
Dreams can be comical, that's for sure!

So if you wander where the wild things play,
Remember the jesters who brighten your day.
Among tangled whispers and forgotten schemes,
Are thickets that bloom with the silliest dreams.

A Ballet of Bramble and Shadow

In the shadowed glen where the brambles prance,
A raccoon named Larry led a strange dance.
With twirls and twists, he flung back his hat,
Stumbling on thorns, imagine that!

The hedgehogs applauded, in emerald hues,
As Larry's slick moves turned into a snooze.
"Oh, what a sight!" said a wise old crow,
"Ballet is tough when the dance floor won't show!"

Then came a fox with two lefty feet,
He stepped on a bramble, oh what a treat!
The brambles giggled, "Is this a grand ball?"
When all turned to chaos, the shadows had a brawl!

With the brambles and critters in wild disarray,
They pirouetted and flopped, in a silly display.
Each thorn a partner, each twig a grand stand,
In this ballet of folly, fun ruled the land.

The Lure of Tangled Thorns

There once was a hedgehog, prickly and pale,
Who fancied himself quite the mythical male.
He sauntered through thorns, chest puffed out proud,
But oops, there he stayed, caught tight in a crowd!

The bumblebees snickered, the wildflowers sighed,
As the hedgehog wiggled and whispered, "I tried!"
With tangles galore, he grinned through the mess,
"Adventure's a blast, even if it's less."

He summoned a rabbit, all nimble and free,
"Help me escape this thorny decree!"
The rabbit hopped over, with laughter in sound,
"Looks like you're stuck, my spiky friend found!"

Yet joy filled the clearing, despite the plight,
For laughter was rampant, shining so bright.
In the lure of the thorns, they all found their song,
Life's quirks are hilarious, and that's where we belong.

Portraits in Plant Life

In a garden of mischief, where greens come to play,
The daisies said, "Let's brighten the day!"
They painted the hedges with splashes of cheer,
While the thorns rolled their eyes, "Oh dear, oh dear!"

Each leaf told a tale, some silly, some wise,
Of critters who slipped, much to their surprise.
The sunflowers grinned, with faces aglow,
"Join in the fun, let your laughter flow!"

"A portrait of chaos, a masterpiece grand,"
Said the willow tree, with a wave of her hand.
But wait—who's that moose, with a hat on his head?
Bumping into petals, "I thought they were bread!"

So here in the garden, embrace the delight,
Where every odd moment is a laughter igniter.
In the portraits of plant life, let joy take its flight,
For the tales of this haven are endlessly bright!

The Silent Watcher of the Wild

In the woods, a squirrel schemes,
Gathering acorns, chasing dreams.
With a twitchy tail and bulging eyes,
He plots his snack with clever lies.

A raccoon waves from a puzzled tree,
"Hey, squirrel, save some for me!"
But with a flick, the squirrel's gone,
Leaving the raccoon all alone.

A wise old owl hoots with glee,
"This game of hide and seek is free!"
Yet in the shadows, shadows play,
And giggles echo in the fray.

So in the wild, where chaos reigns,
Every critter's got funny claims.
They dance and prance with silly quirks,
Making mischief called their work.

Tangled Roots of Memory

A hedgehog snorts, stuck in a vine,
"What's this mess? I thought I'd shine!"
With little feet, he wiggles and plays,
In a jumbled tangle of sunny rays.

An old tortoise laughs, slow as molasses,
"Get out of there before it surpasses!"
But the hedgehog grins, proud of his fight,
"Just part of my charm! I'm a fluffball knight!"

Nearby, a frog croaks a silly tune,
"Come join my band, we'll play till noon!"
With croaks and jumps, they start the show,
Singing of adventures from long ago.

In the thicket where laughter ignites,
Every creature thrives on silly sights.
Through roots and twists, they find their way,
Chasing down memories in a humorous play.

The Hidden Pathways

A snail, with swagger, trots on the trail,
"I may be slow, but I shall not fail!"
With a shiny shell that gleams in the sun,
He's the fastest at heart, just having fun.

Behind a bush, a mouse squeaks bold,
"Careful now, there's treasures untold!"
But the snail just laughs, his pace is grand,
"Every little thing was carefully planned!"

A fluttering butterfly joins the parade,
With colors so bright, it can't be delayed.
"Come on, slowpoke! Let's fly and glide!"
But the snail just smiles, "I'll enjoy the ride."

In the hidden paths where mischief thrives,
Every critter's antics give silly high-fives.
They roam and giggle, no hurries allowed,
In the shuffle of life, they're joyously proud.

Beneath the Canopy of Secrets

A chattering chipmunk plots in the trees,
"Why gather nuts when you can tease?"
With tiny paws, he flicks at the air,
Creating laughter with shenanigans rare.

A wise old crow caws from a height,
"Stop your pranks or you'll start a fight!"
But the chipmunk winks, "I'm just a jester,
Playing my tunes, a fun little tester!"

A fleet-footed deer jumps in delight,
"Let's join the fun, oh, what a sight!"
They leap together with giggles and grace,
In the dappled shade, they've found their place.

So under the leaves where secrets play,
They burst with laughter—come join the fray!
In every rustle, a joke can be found,
Amidst nature's laughter, joy knows no bound.

The Call of the Hidden Haven

In the shade where shadows play,
Squirrels dance and snatch away.
A raccoon with a sly little grin,
Hiding treasure, his cheeky win.

The berries burst with colors bright,
Giggling worms slip out of sight.
A bee in boots jives through the air,
Making sure he spreads some flair.

Frogs enact a comic scene,
Paddle-footed in a dream.
Laughter echoes as they leap,
The secrets of the woods they keep.

In this enclave of leafy fun,
Every critter's race is never done.
With mirth and mischief all around,
Joyous spirits can be found.

Mischief among the Leaves

A rabbit's tickle with a twig,
Sent the fox into a jig.
Underneath the chartreuse haze,
Beneath the canopy of playful praise.

Chirping crickets sing a tune,
While butterflies pirouette like a balloon.
The badger, a jester in this show,
Cracks a joke, watches chuckles grow.

Wily leaves share gossip sly,
As the wind hears them flutter by.
A beetle sidles with much aplomb,
Dressed to impress with shiny charm.

With laughter echoing through the charms,
The woods alive with cheeky arms.
Each corner hides a playful jest,
Where mischief reigns, we feel so blessed.

Life between the Twisted Stems

Twisted stems and tangled vines,
Where a hedgehog hops, and laughter climbs.
A dancing worm in polka dots,
Sways to the rhythm of silly thoughts.

Among the roots, a party forms,
With fireflies lighting up the norms.
A snail strikes a pose, not a care,
Mellow mood with the night to share.

The frisky mice, they twirl about,
Caught in fun without a doubt.
With every squeak, they burst with glee,
Together in dreams, so wild and free.

In this realm of twisted plot,
Every creature knows their spot.
Life's a hoot with every twist,
A rollicking dance, too fun to miss!

Whimsy in the Wild Bower

In the bower, whimsy reigns,
Where porcupines wear their thorny chains.
A dandy lizard struts with pride,
Under colorful petals, he cannot hide.

Chubby robins play peek-a-boo,
Bouncing 'round like coffee brew.
The sunbeams tickle the leaves so bright,
Creating shadows that giggle in flight.

A toadstool tosses a cheeky grin,
As beetles celebrate with a din.
A merry band of playful rogues,
Singing songs as twilight bogs.

In this whimsical, vibrant den,
Bouncing laughter, again and again.
Every nook a secret joke,
In the wild bower, dreams provoke.

The Enchanted Bramble Path

Once I stumbled on a trail,
Where bushes waved and tried to wail.
The thorns proposed a prickly dance,
Each step a chance for mischief's chance.

A squirrel offered me a seat,
And chewed on nuts, a savory treat.
I slipped on moss, but laughed instead,
For even the trees just rolled their heads.

The hedgehogs giggled in a row,
As I tripped over roots, oh no!
Their laughter rang like tiny bells,
In this wild place where fun dwells.

Whiskers twitched with every joke,
A ladybug gave me a poke.
With each misstep, the sun shone bright,
In this merry land of jovial fright.

Hidden Songs of the Overgrowth

In the shade where the funny flies,
The plants hold secrets, to my surprise.
A snail gave me a wink and a smile,
Said, "Stick around, let's chat a while!"

The daisies danced in a silly way,
And beckoned me to join their play.
A bumblebee led a merry parade,
While I just watched, without a charade.

The mushrooms hummed a silly tune,
That made me think of a clumsy moon.
With each pitter-patter of paws around,
A ruckus of joy could surely be found.

A toad croaked out his jolly refrain,
As I laughed with glee, not a hint of pain.
Surrounded by fun, oh what a sight,
Nature's laughter, a pure delight!

Whispers of Rustic Dreams

Under leaves with a cheeky grin,
A chipmunk whispered, "Come on in!"
Rusty dreams danced in my head,
With squirrels plotting, oh what a thread!

The cobwebs sparkled with morning dew,
Like fairy lights in a bizarre zoo.
A frog in a crown proclaimed with flair,
"Join my court, if you dare!"

Butterflies giggled, swirling around,
While chaos of blooms painted the ground.
They held a concert, nature's delight,
Where every twig wanted to take flight.

Laughter bubbled from echoes unseen,
As nature's stage shared a whimsical scene.
Each rustling leaf held a playful theme,
In this wild land of rustic dreams.

Tales from the Twilit Thicket

In the thicket as dusk drew near,
A cast of critters appeared, my dear.
Raccoons played cards near a gnarled tree,
While badgers toasted to a wild spree.

A shadow snickered, a ghostly hare,
Claiming he'd once tried to do a hair.
He miscalculated the length of his furs,
And ended up with a hat of blurs!

The owls debated who won last night,
Arguing endlessly, a comical sight.
They cawed and hooted, oh what a scene,
Their wise old heads a jolly machine.

Every tale told brought laughter and cheer,
In the twilit embrace, no room for fear.
With nature's jesters and spirits around,
The magic of humor was joyfully found!

Whispers of Woven Shadows

In the thicket where shadows play,
A squirrel juggles nuts all day.
With acorns bouncing, what a sight,
Even the bumblebees take flight.

The rabbits gossip, tails in a twist,
While frogs practice leaping, none can resist.
A hedgehog slips, with a comical wiggle,
Even the thorns seem to giggle and jiggle.

A fox in a hat, struts with a flair,
As the owls roll their eyes, unaware.
The trees join in, with whispers of fun,
Under their branches, mischief has run.

And so the woodland weaves its tale,
Of nutty chases and wild, funny trails.
With laughter hidden in leaves so green,
It's the quirkiest place you'd ever seen.

Tangled Stories of the Wild

In a maze where the wild creatures roam,
A cat tells tales of a kingdom, her home.
With dogs as knights, and birds as spies,
Every story brings giggles and sighs.

The badgers debate, with a serious air,
While the raccoons plot with nary a care.
"Let's steal some snacks!" they all chant as one,
As the chipmunks shout, "Oh, this will be fun!"

The peacock prances, flaunting his tail,
While the field mice tune in to the tale.
A hedgehog raises an eyebrow with glee,
"Let's see if this ends with a cup of tea!"

With a twist and a turn, the yarns are spun,
In the underbrush where laughter is done.
The tangled stories, wild and free,
Bring joy to each heart in the leafy spree.

Secrets in the Underbrush

In the thicket where giggles reside,
A frog tells secrets, old as the tide.
With whispers of mischief, he croaks with delight,
As ladybugs listen, well into the night.

The hedgehogs gather, hats on their snouts,
Swapping their tales, and giving out shouts.
A shy little mouse shares a humorous fall,
While worms roll their eyes, thinking she's small.

A fox with a grin, spinning his yarn,
Claims he's the hero, reacting with charm.
But the truth is a twist, as the turtles inquire,
"Wonder if foxes can truly retire?"

Under the leaves, where the secrets hide,
The laughter erupts, an infectious tide.
Each story a treasure, each giggle a gem,
In the underbrush where fun's on a whim.

The Depths of the Thicket

In the depths of the thicket, where chaos abounds,
The creatures are plotting in whimsical rounds.
A badger in glasses reads from a book,
While a gang of young weasels are getting a look.

They practice their schemes, with a flick of the tail,
While owls hoot advice, never too frail.
"Let's disguise as flowers, then sneak past the cat!"
Their laughter erupts, as they schemed and spat.

A porcupine slips, with a squeak of surprise,
But the chipmunks all cheer, "You'll win this, you'll rise!"
As the thicket erupts with camaraderie's cheer,
The woodland's own sitcom is joyfully here.

With contests of silliness, joy is the key,
In the depths where the critters feel wild and free.
So let's raise a toast with a splash in the air,
To laughter and tales, no worries or care.

The Cradle of Wayward Boughs

In the cradle where wild things sway,
A squirrel chats as if to say,
"Watch your head, dear friend, take care!"
While dodging branches plump and rare.

Outside the reach of normal life,
A hedgehog plots with flair and strife,
His prickly hat, so full of pride,
Rolls down the path, just trying to hide.

Ladybugs wear spots like clothes,
While beetles dance, and caterpillars pose,
They laugh at gnomes who sit and pout,
Just wishing they could join the rout.

In this place of whimsical cheer,
Nature whispers nothing to fear,
So let's join in this crazy spree,
Where oddities are always free!

Serenity in the Scrub

Through tangled roots and leaves galore,
A frog performs on a mossy floor,
"Ribbit, ribbit! Join my dance!"
While bees create a buzzing trance.

A shy old fox, with a crooked grin,
Steals a berry, where to begin?
The blueberries simply burst with glee,
Squeezed by tiny, joyful feet.

A dandelion spins tales of flight,
Of wishes made on a warm summer night,
As rabbits hop with laughter bright,
Chasing shadows till the light.

Here, serenity's not all that serious,
Amidst the quirky, oh so curious,
Every creature knows quite well,
Here, life's a whimsical carousel!

Connections among the Creepers

Vines intertwine like old friends ever tight,
Playing games with the sun 'til night,
A chameleon's giggle, a mouse's cheer,
Creating connections, just over here!

The playful lizard, in shades of green,
Dances with shadows, a clever routine,
"Catch me if you can!" it shouts with glee,
As crickets play the tune, whee!

Mushrooms offer shade with a goofy stance,
While ants march on in a regimented prance,
"Next stop is dinner!" they all declare,
Ambitious travelers, full of flair!

Among these creepers, life thrives anew,
With laughter stitched in each shaded hue,
For in this realm of playful jest,
Connections blossom, never a rest!

Remnants of the Untamed Path

In the land where the wild things roam,
Pebbles trip on their way back home,
Thistles grin with their prickly might,
Winking at passersby in delight.

A wandering bee wears a crown of fluff,
Buzzing songs of happiness that feels tough,
Yet in his heart, there's a playful glee,
Causing flowers to blush with the honey spree.

Worms throw parties beneath the ground,
Confetti of soil sprinkled all around,
They dance when raindrops loudly cheer,
Celebrating life's jest, with scrumptious beer.

So here on this path where chaos meets,
Every misstep brings forth funny feats,
For those who wander, chuckle on their way,
Embracing each twist, here's where they play!

Where Shadows Dance with Light

In the woods where shadows play,
A squirrel stole my snack today.
He winked at me with nuts in hand,
A furry thief, so bold and grand.

The sun sneezed through the leafy trees,
Tickling all with a gentle breeze.
While I tripped on a root, fell down,
The shadows giggled all around.

A rabbit hopped and spun in glee,
Made a crown of leaves for me.
We danced in circles, all a-flutter,
Until I landed in the gutter.

With laughter ringing, off we sped,
A game of tag, I lost my head!
Yet in the light, oh what a sight,
Where shadows skip from day to night.

Heartbeats of the Woodland

The trees are tapping their little feet,
To a rhythm that's wild and sweet.
A woodpecker plays the drum,
While a hedgehog strums, oh what fun!

A wise old owl in a funky cap,
Watches us swirl in a woodland lap.
The fox joins in with a dapper dance,
While I trip over a root, no chance!

Frogs croak out a goofy tune,
Underneath a bright fat moon.
We bounce and hop, twirl about,
With woodland beats, there's no doubt.

So if you're feeling a bit out of sync,
Join the creatures, stop, and think.
The heart of the woods is loud and bright,
Let's groove with nature, a silly sight!

Lost in a Tangle

Oh what a mess this path has made,
With vines and twigs in a leafy cascade.
A raccoon waved as I stumbled in,
He giggled loud, winked with a grin.

Caught in a thicket, I spun around,
Thought I had found treasure abound.
But all I got was a thistle poke,
From a prickly friend with a mean joke.

An ant marched by, wearing a hat,
Said, "You're quite lost, and that's a fact!"
I laughed and danced in the tangle tight,
With critters joining, all feeling right.

We laughed at the topsy-turvy scene,
In this wild maze, oh so keen.
Though I came for berries, I left with cheer,
In the tangled woods, I felt no fear.

The Silent Embrace of Thorns

In a bramble bush, I found a seat,
Where thorns and laughter make a treat.
A hedgehog chuckled, said, "Stay a while,"
As flowers nodded, dressed with style.

Roses blushed, their petals bright,
While thorns whispered secrets by moonlight.
"Be careful here," the flowers said,
But I just giggled, ignoring dread.

A bumblebee buzzed in with flair,
Wearing a tiny, golden pair.
He bumped my nose, then stole my toast,
What a picnic, I love to boast!

In this prickle patch, I found delight,
With every poke and every bite.
So here I stay, not in a hurry,
In thorny laughter, there's no worry.

In the Fold of Nature's Bequest

In a patch where critters dance,
A squirrel in tights begins to prance.
With acorns piled high like a feast,
He juggles with glee, a furry beast.

The hedgehogs roll in a pushy spree,
Competing for snacks with an old bumblebee.
While frogs croak tunes that make the mice giggle,
A rabbit pops up, doing a wiggly wiggle.

Badgers in bow ties strut with pride,
Giving etiquette lessons on the side.
While ducks wear hats that are far too big,
Declaring they're out for a fancy gig.

In this leafy land where laughter reigns,
The creatures unite, dancing in chains.
So if you wander, bring a smile,
For nature's antics stretch a whole mile!

The Confluence of Shadows and Light

Where shadows mingle, the sun takes tea,
A chipmunk complains, "I can't find my key!"
The dance of the leaves, a jig so bright,
Twists a tale of giggles, both day and night.

A raccoon slips on an old banana peel,
And rolls down a hill, oh what a deal!
While crickets compose a symphonic hum,
A beetle joins in with a tiny drum.

The sunbeams tickle the grass, so spry,
As butterflies flutter, teaching how to fly.
Singing songs of mischief, young sparrows take flight,
Turning every moment into pure delight.

And shadows chuckle while they appear,
In this patch of laughter, all are sincere.
Join the parade of giggles and fun,
Where laughter blooms like the rays of the sun!

Serenity of the Wild Thicket

In the thick of it all, a party ensues,
With owls in pajamas and hedgehogs in shoes.
They sip on sweet nectar from flower to flower,
Exchanging tall tales of nature's own power.

The beetles play chess on a leaf shaped like gold,
While butterflies gossip, their wings uncontrolled.
A fox brings the snacks, a spread quite unique,
Salads of mushrooms with berries to leak.

The sun sets softly, a DJ of dusk,
With fireflies twinkling; it's quite the husk.
As shadows grow longer, the laughter grows loud,
In this thicket of jokes where joy is avowed.

So give a hoot, and dance without care,
For nature's a stage, and we're all in the air.
With whims and with smiles, let's all share the night,
In this serene spot, everything feels right!

The Guardian of the Hidden Hollow

In a hollow well-hidden, a legend lives large,
An owl on a throne, the king of the charge.
He wears a crown made of twigs and of leaves,
And rules over critters with hilarious beliefs.

His subjects, a chorus of squirrels and shrews,
Throw parties on branches, inviting the blues.
They dance through the treetops, in outfits quite rare,
While toads lead the band with a style beyond compare.

"Who needs a treasure when you've got good cheer?"
Said the wise guardian, "Let's toast with some beer!"
With acorns as glasses, they all gave a cheer,
Underneath the stars, their laughter sincere.

So if you find a path that twists and that winds,
Know joy is waiting, the best of all kinds.
For in this hidden hollow, where silliness reigns,
Every creature is welcome; everyone gains!

The Calm of the Shaded Sanctuary

In the coolness of shade, so serene,
A squirrel lost his acorn, quite the scene.
He searched under leaves, in a frantic dance,
While bees laughed aloud at his clumsy prance.

Here lies a napkin, all wrinkled and torn,
The picnic leftovers, forgotten at dawn.
A raccoon now feasts, with a grin on his face,
As birds pass around, they giggle, retrace.

Under a tree, the wise owl would hoot,
He claims it's a meeting of all the cute.
But really it's chaos, a jumbled affair,
Of laughter and chatter, filled up with fresh air.

So come take a seat, where the sun meets the fun,
Join in the mayhem, you're not the only one.
In the calm of this place, with antics around,
A humor-filled trip can surely be found.

Enclave of the Lost Petal

In a nook filled with quirks, petals fall down,
One mischievous breeze keeps swirling around.
It juggles old spoons and the occasional shoe,
Making the flowers break out in a view.

A ladybug slips on a petal so bright,
As butterflies cheer in pure delight.
A snail races by, on a note he must glide,
While thorns shake their heads, too prickly for pride.

The laughter of weeds, with their witty remarks,
Share stories of gardens where chaos embarks.
While daisies gossip, just off to the side,
They nod to the gossip that they can't abide.

In this enclave of petals, the humor runs free,
Where nothing is serious, just chaos and glee.
So gather your thoughts, let your worries take flight,
In the land of lost petals, the world's just right.

The Harmony of Vines and Shadows

Under a canopy of tangled old vines,
The shadows play tricks, drawing silly lines.
A rabbit hops in, wearing socks that don't match,
His fashion a marvel, they'll never catch!

The mushrooms are chatting, with tops worn so proud,
While ferns flick their fronds, with whimsy aloud.
A chubby old toad croaks a nonsensical tune,
As crickets join in with the light of the moon.

Each branch holds a secret that giggles and sighs,
As whispers of mischief flow down from the skies.
A slug steals the spotlight, a comedian's dream,
While hedgehogs all chuckle, they know just the theme.

In this harmony rich, where giggles entwine,
Every moment is filled with jest on a vine.
So dance with the shadows, let laughter take flight,
In the company of vines, the world is just right.

Grove of the Eternal Twist

In the grove where the trees are always askew,
A parrot tells tales of two turtles who flew.
With a wink and a nod, they tripped on their feet,
And landed in bushes, now isn't that sweet?

A hedgehog in glasses reads books on a stump,
Deciding each plot is just one big jump.
He scribbles his thoughts with a laugh as he twirls,
Declaring it's time for a party for squirrels.

The sun it peeks in through the branches alive,
As bees break the news that they're starting a jive.
While raccoons prepare, with their shiny new hats,
Proclaiming they're ready to welcome the cats!

In this grove filled with laughter, all twisty and mad,
Every critter dancing, both happy and glad.
So join in the fun, let your worries crowd out,
In the grove of the twist, all joy is about!

In the Heart of the Overgrowth

A squirrel with a sense of flair,
Found a hat that fit just right.
He danced beneath the tangled hair,
And gave the bushes quite a fright.

The rabbit joined with floppy ears,
In heels that made him skip and slide.
They giggled loud, ignored their fears,
And paraded forth with dreams of pride.

A hedgehog tried to twirl and twist,
But pricked himself, oh what a sight!
He laughed and said, "Can't resist,
Next time I'll do this in twilight!"

Underneath a sun so bright,
The party grew amid the greens.
With every hop, they took their flight,
And shared their wild secretive schemes.

Songs of the Wild Aspirant

A raccoon sang a tune so bold,
About the trash can's hidden gold.
With each high note, the bees would buzz,
And dance along because they must.

He dreamt one day to steal a glance,
At every party, start a chance,
But tripped on roots while doing so,
And sent a hedgehog to and fro.

A chorus formed of leafy friends,
Who harmonized and made amends.
They laughed at hiccups in the tune,
And vowed to practice 'neath the moon.

The forest echoed with their glee,
As critters crooned in wild unity.
Each song a dream, a little jest,
Amid the boughs, they found their zest.

The Dance of the Wildwood Shadows

In shadows where the critters creep,
A party starts without a peep.
A lizard twirls, a moth takes flight,
While leaves ignite the starry night.

A shimmering brook joins in the fun,
With splashes that make everyone run.
The owl hoots at the sparkly scene,
While fireflies flash in a glow so keen.

Each critter laughs, no fears in sight,
As twigs and berries lend delight.
One hedgehog slipped, fell on his face,
But shrugged and found a funky grace.

The dance was wild, the best they say,
With each moonlit sway, they lost their way.
In nature's art, they'd play their part,
While shadows painted joy in heart.

A Journey through the Green Maze

In ivy nests where dreams unfurl,
A dandy beetle gave a twirl.
He lost his way, turned left, then right,
And found himself in quite a plight.

A wise old snail with much to say,
Offered tips to find the way.
"Just keep your eyes on shiny things,
And watch for nests where laughter sings!"

Around the corners, they did race,
Each twist and turn a funny face.
A thistle prickle stole the show,
As giggles echoed high and low.

Together through the lush array,
With silly jokes, they spent the day.
In every leaf and winding path,
They found their joy, they found their laugh.

Enigmas Wrapped in Foliage

A squirrel wore a tiny hat,
He danced with glee, oh what of that.
A riddle hid beneath a vine,
While mushrooms giggled, oh so fine.

The branches swayed, the leaves they chuckled,
A whispering breeze, it softly snuggled.
The shadows laughed, they had a jest,
As acorns bounced, they seemed quite blessed.

In every nook, a secret hid,
The groundhog shared a dance, he did.
With twigs and thorns as marionettes,
The plants staged plays, no one forgets.

So if you stroll among the green,
Just know there's mischief, yet unseen.
For nature's charm is quite a hoot,
A jolly jingle in each root.

Under the Canopy's Secret

A rabbit wore a little coat,
He tiptoed soft, a sneaky note.
The owls blinked and winked with charm,
While beetles piled on leafy arm.

Each branch held laughter, wild and bright,
In whispers shared throughout the night.
The hedgehog told a joke so bold,
About a bee, who loved the cold.

A fox played cards with ladybugs,
He lost his bets to tiny shrugs.
The sunlight glimmered, twinkled loud,
As shadows joined the merry crowd.

In tangled roots, a secret's hue,
Is laughter shared, just me and you.
So grab a friend, explore and cheer,
For all the jesters gather here.

Dances of the Wildflower Glade

In wildflower fields, a party sprung,
With daisies twirling, joy was hung.
The butterflies flapped, a lively cheer,
While teasing breezes whispered near.

A bee in shades did strut and sway,
A ladybug joined the grand ballet.
With petals bright, the dance did flow,
The mushrooms tapped their feet, you know.

As grasshoppers chirped their jazzy beat,
The flowers wiggled on nimble feet.
Each bloom had stories, quirks to boast,
Of bees' wild dreams, they'd raise a toast.

So take a step in this floral spread,
Leave worries behind, just dance instead.
For every petal holds a song,
In this wild glade where laughs belong.

Buried Dreams beneath Foliage

In tangled roots, dreams take their rest,
A gopher grinned, he claimed the best.
With whispers soft from crickets near,
A treasure map, a fun frontier.

Amid the brambles, what to find?
A recipe for sunshine, unconfined.
The snails conspired with the toad,
To bake a cake from forest road.

With twigs like forks, they dined in style,
And told tall tales with flair and guile.
The trees above, they leaned and swayed,
To catch a glimpse of this charade.

So if you peek among the green,
You'll find grand quests, oh so unseen.
For underneath the leafy frame,
Are buried dreams that dance with fame.

Hidden Realm of the Overgrown

In the garden where weeds plot,
A snail meets a shoe, a curious thought.
The branches chat with a giggle and sway,
While squirrels argue who's winning the day.

A mushroom wears a crown of bright red,
Complaining of thorns, tired of being wed.
The grasses dance, a ballet with flair,
While daisies giggle at the sun's bright glare.

Rabbits wear glasses, reading their maps,
While fireflies wink at the napping chaps.
The hedgehog insists he's still in the race,
While frogs croak loudly, just keeping pace.

In this thicket of laughter, what fun to explore,
As nature reveals secrets we can't ignore.
With each twist and turn, there's humor to find,
In the wild and the wacky, we leave stress behind.

Thorns That Sing

Thorns strum a tune on a trumpet leaf,
Their melodies rise, a jaunty motif.
The bramble bushes hum, what a sight,
As bees join the chorus, buzzing with delight.

A ladybug dances, quite sure of her style,
Waltzing with thorns, they celebrate a while.
A caterpillar spins tales of woe,
But the thorns just chuckle, 'Come join our show!'

The bumblebees bicker, in rhythm they prance,
While some hippo grass starts a rhyming romance.
The sun shines bright, with a mischievous wink,
In a patch of hilarity, they laugh and they stink.

So next time you wander where the wild things sing,
Remember the jest in nature's grand fling.
For in each thorn's whisper, a secret is wrapped,
A chuckle awaits where the wild is untapped.

Refuge of the Wandering Mind

In the nook where the lost thoughts play,
A butterfly loiters, enjoying the day.
The mushrooms debate in philosophic tones,
While shadows of laughter dance on the stones.

A wild hare scribbles poetry in the dirt,
Introducing wild ideas without a shirt.
The vines entwine with a comical bow,
As hedges gossip about time's funny how.

The wind whispers secrets to trees with a grin,
A joke about acorns that keeps them all in.
The flowers burst forth, painting the air,
With vivid confessions of love and despair.

In this refuge, each whimsy finds space,
As jesters of nature add joy to the chase.
So roam through the wild, let your troubles unwind,
In the refuge of pranks from the wandering mind.

Tales from the Hidden Fold

In a fold of the green, where good vibes abound,
The rabbits concoct a tale that's renowned.
With carrots as swords and lettuce for shields,
Epic battles unfold on fantastical fields.

The fox tells a story, a bit out of hand,
Of a chicken who dreamed of a rock 'n' roll band.
The turtles debate who's the fastest of all,
As a brave little mouse joins their curious call.

Jokes ricochet off the boughs in a whirl,
While flowers giggle and begin to unfurl.
A dancing beetle waltzes with flair,
As grapevines twist, creating a snare.

From hidden folds, laughter spills to the sky,
With every adventure, we joyfully fly.
So join in this realm where the silly is gold,
For tales from the thicket are whimsically bold.

The Choir of Hidden Blossoms

A bloom in a tangle, what a sight,
They giggle and wiggle in morning light.
With petals like hats, they'll sing a tune,
As bumblebees dance, they'll sway 'til noon.

Their colors are bold, a comical show,
Each flower with jokes that only they know.
They plan a parade through the green and gray,
While ants form a band—hip-hip-hooray!

A daisy with glasses declares it's time,
To order a lunch of sweet, gooey slime.
Tulips get tipsy on nectar supreme,
And sunflower heads nod to the wildest dream.

So join this fine mess of petals and leaves,
Where laughter erupts and nothing deceives.
In gardens of giggles, they frolic and play,
With smiles that bloom brighter each glorious day.

Among the Ferns of Forgotten Tales

In the ferns, secrets poke just a bit,
They whisper of shadows where critters sit.
An old toad is rapping, a snail's got the beat,
While crickets and beetles are dancing on feet.

Each frond has a story, each curl has a laugh,
As they plot an escape from the gardener's path.
The twigs start to snap, it's a game of hide-and-seek,
With cheers from the leaves that are cheeky and meek.

A fairy forgets her drink, oh dear me!
She sips on some dew that was meant for a bee.
And mushrooms arise for a tea party sweet,
With laughter like bubbles that pop at your feet.

So wander through green, take a guess at the fun,
Where memories laugh in the shade of the sun.
With ferns as your guides, let the stories unveil,
As every step leads to a curious tale.

Veils of Moss and Memory

Moss sheets like blankets on rocks with a grin,
Hiding tales of critters that dance and spin.
A squirrel in socks tries a waltz on a log,
While mushrooms erupt like a well-timed fog.

The whispers of moss tell of decades gone by,
Where shadows wore crowns, and the tall grasses sigh.
A porcupine's pondering a career in mime,
As the sunlight giggles at old tales of crime.

A ladybug plotted her rogue butterfly scheme,
To rule over daisies and live like a dream.
But confusion ensued as she tripped on a sprout,
While the ants in the back laughed and shouted, "Get out!"

So meander along these soft emerald trails,
Who knows what you'll find in the whispers and wails?
For veils of the past, both silly and sweet,
Invite you to join in this joke-filled retreat.

The Mystery of Twisted Limbs

In the woods where the limbs twist and twirl,
A raccoon is caught in a red scarf swirl.
Branches debate if they're really that crooked,
While squirrels make fashion of nuts they've cookied.

Oh, the trouble they make in their tangled up games,
Where snapping twigs shout like exuberant names.
A woodpecker cackles at all of the fuss,
While chipmunks conspire to ride on a bus.

And in all of this chaos, the sun starts to beam,
Casting shadows that dance like a wacky dream.
An owl with a monocle watches with glee,
As the woods fall in laughter, alive and carefree.

So step into this plot where the limbs misbehave,
Where the tales twist and turn in a wobbly wave.
For in the green maze of whimsy and fun,
The mystery beckons, let's giggle and run!

www.ingramcontent.com/pod-product-compliance
Lightning Source LLC
Chambersburg PA
CBHW072118070526
44585CB00016B/1492